When I was editorial dire[ ] always count on Marlene Bagnull to write biblical, practical, and powerful personal experience stories for us. Here are her step by step secrets to having over a thousand of her manuscripts published.

James N. Watkins
Award-winning book and article author

Do you need tips on how to tell your story in a way that will transform lives, change minds, or renew hope? It's time to dive into Marlene Bagnull's latest book, *How to Write His Answer, Testimonies and Personal Experience Stories.* Marlene shares incredible storytelling secrets so that the stories of your life can make a lasting impact.

Linda Evans Shepherd
Founder, Advanced Writers & Speakers Association
Best-selling author, *When You Don't Know What to Pray*
and *Praying God's Promises*

In these pages you'll discover an experienced writing coach who is interested in helping you tell your stories. If you want to respond to your Heavenly Father's call to "Write His Answer," this practical resource is the perfect starting point. Brimming with real examples and easy to follow instructions that will encourage you to take the next step in your writing ministry.

Sue Cameron
Author, *Hope, Healing and Help for Survivors of Sexual*
Abuse: A Faith-based Journey to Healing*

Few have the experience of Marlene Bagnull to teach writers and to give writers the tools they need to *Write His Answer* and to do it so well. These are practical items even experienced writers need reminding of, such as: have a clear focus, stay close to the Lord, search for truth, reflect (and journal) on *your* life experiences, stay humble, know your audiences—all of this to remind us that we, as believers in the Lord Jesus, are called to write *His* answer to those with so many questions. Written conversationally, this book invites you to take part in the work with a ready pen.

Eva Marie Everson
Bestselling & multiple award-winning author & speaker
President, Word Weavers International

If you want solid, sound advice on writing, Marlene Bagnull is the authority you're looking for.

Gayle Roper
Lost and Found, Hide and Seek

In this first book in Marlene Bagnull's *How to Write His Answer* series, you'll discover (or rediscover!) the eight elements needed to write for Jesus. Though titled, "Testimonies and Personal Experience Stories," this book's content applies to all our writing, for if we cannot share our own story, how can we share any other story? Thick with encouragement and wisdom, you'll refer back to this guide over and over, for it reveals God's path for writers, whatever your topic.

Patricia Durgin
Marketing Expert and Trainer
Founder, Marketers On A Mission

Personal Experience & Testimonies is the perfect kick-off for Marlene's *How to Write His Answer* series. Why? Because our lives are built on experiences with God that can help and inspire others, and what better starting place? Marlene has condensed the best nuggets of her multi-decade mentoring of Christian writers into this handy book. Follow her lead and get your much-needed personal story out there. Only you can tell it.

Candy Abbott
Owner, Fruitbearer Publishing LLC

Marlene is the godmother of Christian writing, having encouraged, motivated, and blessed Christian writers for decades. Her seminars, conferences, and writings have helped launch a thousand ships that have in turn blessed the world. The words in this book are solidly rooted in Scripture, molded by practical wisdom, and bathed in prayer.

David Rupert
***Patheos* columnist**
Author of *Living a Life of Yes*

There are two things that are of vital importance to Marlene— her relationship to the Father and encouraging Christian writers. Both are evident in the pages of this book. *How to Write His Answer* is a wonderful blend of inspirational and practical. It is a must-read for someone looking to encourage others through their own life's story.

M. Esther Lovejoy
Author, *The Sweet Side of Suffering*

How to
Write
His
Answer

Testimonies and Personal Experience Stories

With Links to 4 Audio Workshops

Marlene Bagnull

Ampelos Press

How to Write His Answer: Testimonies & Personal Experience Stories
Includes links to four workshops downloadable as MP3s.

© 2020 by Marlene
Bagnull ISBN:
978-0-9821653-5-5

Published by Ampelos Press, 951 Anders Road, Lansdale, PA 19446
https://writehisanswer.com/Ampelospressbooks, mbagnull@aol.com

"The Power of Your Story" originally published in *The Complete Guide to Christian Writing and Speaking.* Susan Titus Osborn, General Editor. Second Edition, WriteNow Publications, 2001.

"Going & Growing through the Hurts," "Writing Your Testimony," and "Finding Your Place" originally published in *Write His Answer – A Bible Study for Christian Writers* by Marlene Bagnull. Third Edition, Ampelos Press, 2014.

"Words," page 57, © copyright 1993 Sue Cameron. Used by permission.

Unless otherwise noted all Scripture quotations are taken from The Living Bible copyright © 1971 by Tyndale House Foundation. Used by permission of Tyndale House Publishers Inc., Carol Stream, Illinois 60188. All rights reserved. The Living Bible, TLB, and The Living Bible logo are registered trademarks of Tyndale House Publishers.

Scripture quotations marked NIV are taken from the Holy Bible, New International Version®, NIV®. Copyright ©1973, 1978, 1984, 2011 by Biblica, Inc.™ Used by permission of Zondervan. All rights reserved worldwide. www.zondervan.com The "NIV" and "New International Version" are trademarks registered in the United States Patent and Trademark Office by Biblica, Inc.™

Scripture quotations marked KJV are taken from the *King James Version.*

Printed in the United States of America

To those
Father has called
to
"Write His Answer"

Table of Contents

And the Lord said to me,
"Write my answer on a billboard,
large and clear,
so that anyone can read it at a glance
and rush to tell the others."

Habakkuk 2:2

1

The Power of Your Story

His usual method of teaching
was to tell the people stories.
MARK 4:2

"There was a man who had two sons. The younger one said to his father, 'Father, give me my share of the estate . . .'" In essence: "I want what's coming to me *now!*"

So begins one of Jesus' most remembered and loved stories, recorded for us in Luke 15:11-32. We remember it because it speaks to us. We love it because it gives us hope whether we're a parent waiting for a prodigal to come home, a prodigal who wonders if he will be welcomed home, or the older brother (or sister) who feels unappreciated and unloved.

Jesus frequently told stories because He knew it was one of the best ways He could connect with people. I believe He is telling us to "go and do likewise."

How can we effectively harness the power of the story to reach our listeners and readers? By telling and writing the stories we know best—our own personal stories of how we came to know Christ and the difference He is making in our lives.

Maybe it's because I really don't enjoy research, or maybe it's because as my mentor frequently told me, I have so much grist (problems) for my writing and speaking mill. Whatever the reason, almost from the beginning of my writing and speaking ministry, I've drawn on my personal experiences. Not only am I convinced that it's one of the most powerful ways to minister to others, it's also a way I can live out the "all things work together for good" promise. You see, if even one person is helped through my experience, my struggle has not been in vain and the evil one is not the victor.

Now please don't misunderstand what I'm saying. I don't like problems! The truth is, I'd much rather run from problems than face them, but running usually isn't an option. It doesn't help that problems are groupies. Seriously, when was the last time you had only *one* problem you needed to solve? Problems rarely come singly. Instead, they seem to gang up on us until we feel surrounded and overwhelmed.

"Why, God?" is a question people frequently ask. But Jesus never promised us a problem-free life. What He has promised is always to be with us. That's the message people need to hear, and that's the message we have the privilege of sharing as writers and speakers. But how can we share it effectively? How can we harness the power of the story?

Keep a Journal

Although we are convinced that we'll *never* forget the details of what happened or the intensity of our feelings, we will! Time is a wonderful healer of memories. We also seem to have a propensity for remembering the wrong things and forgetting what we need to remember. I call it the "I'd Rather Go Back to Egypt" syndrome. Parents who are hoarse from repeating themselves, call it selective listening/remembering.

What's the remedy? Keep a journal! Not a journal that becomes a ball and chain that creates all sorts of guilt when you don't write in it, but a journal that is used to capture the lessons God is teaching you so you don't forget them— and don't need to repeat them over and over!

Journaling will help you "write from the heart as well as from the head," Luci Shaw said in *Life Path*: *Personal and Spiritual Growth through Journal Writing* (Regent College Publishing, 2004).

If journaling isn't for you, write letters and keep copies. Confiding in people on paper is a wonderful way to work through problems. Email makes it even easier to write and save your thoughts. Set your system to automatically save what you send and sort it into folders according to subject. When the time comes to write and speak on a problem you've faced and overcome, you'll have a wealth of material to draw from.

Inventory and Reflect On Your Life Experiences

Some experiences are best not shared. Let's face it. Our listeners and readers really aren't interested in all the boring details of our lives. Nor are they likely to be interested in our family tree. But I guarantee they will be interested in the times God lifted us "out of the pit of despair, out from the bog and the mire" and set our feet on a "hard, firm path" (Psalm 40:2). When we sing that new song of praise to Him, many "will stand in awe before the Lord, and put their trust in him" (Psalm 40:3).

One important principle—don't tell or write it too soon. When we're still in the midst, it's best to share our experiences only with our journal and a close friend—not an audience of strangers. Our readers and listeners want to be able to look to us for answers—answers we can't give them if we're stick stuck in the bog and the mire.

Does that mean we have to totally work through a problem and be walking in complete victory before we speak or write about it?

I'm sure that's what the adversary wants us to believe, for if that were the case, groups would never be able to find speakers, and there would be few books in print. But have we gotten far enough on the other side of the problem to have gained some perspective? If we're still trying to gain a toehold to climb out of the pit, we can't pull anyone else out.

One experience all Christians need to be prepared to share is our salvation testimony. But perhaps you grew up in a Christian home, always went to Sunday school and church, and can't remember a time when you didn't believe. Does that mean you don't have a testimony to share? Of course not!

Although you may not have a dramatic testimony of how God saved you, no doubt you do have many stories of things God has been teaching you throughout your life journey. These stories may have a far greater impact on the believer who is struggling to live out his or her faith in the midst of the daily grind.

Let's face it. The real testing ground for our faith is in the events of everyday life. We know we need the Lord when big problems hit, but all too often we may try to handle on our own the little things that catch us off guard or try our patience. For instance, how may of us have no business advertising we're a Christian on the bumper stickers of our cars when we are anything but a positive witness behind the wheel?

Check Your Heart

"We can be mirrors that brightly reflect the glory of the Lord," the apostle Paul says in 2 Corinthians 3:18. We need to ask ourselves if that is, indeed, our goal when we pick up our pen or stand up to speak. Remember that both our arms (and our readers and listeners) will get bent out of shape if we're intent on patting ourselves on the back. Our goal needs to be to point the readers to God, not to ourselves.

Humility is not only a virtue, it's a necessity for writers and speakers. "Do not exalt yourself or set yourself up as the perfect example of trust in action…. Remember, that your reader cannot identify with, or take advice from, a know-it-all," Ethel Herr said in her classic book, *An Introduction to Christian Writing* (ACW Press, 2001).

"And all of you serve each other with humble spirits," the apostle Peter advises, "for God gives special blessings to those who are humble, but sets himself against those who are proud" (1 Peter 5:5). What a terrifying thing it would be to have God set Himself against us! We dare not let our press releases go to our head.

While we can fool men, we can never fool God. He knows the motives of our hearts. May we never forget that our Lord didn't come to be served, but to serve others. If we want to one day hear Him say, "Well done, good and faithful servant!" (Matthew 25:23 NIV), fame and fortune cannot be our goal.

Know Your Audience

Taking the time to find out as much as you can about your audience is one of the best ways to make certain your story will speak to their needs.

What is their average age? Are they single, married, or divorced? Do they have children and, if so, are their children infants or toddlers, school age or grown? Is your audience both male and female? Are they primarily high school or college graduates, professional or blue collar? And, so as not to unwittingly step on toes, if you're speaking to a church group or writing for a denominational magazine, what are their basic tenets of faith? Can you speak or write to them without feeling compelled to try and change their beliefs?

The business world spends thousands of dollars on market research before developing and releasing a new product. Shouldn't we at least spend some time in researching our audience? Once we identify who we are "targeting," we can take better "aim" by praying for them and seeking the Lord for the message He would have us bring to them.

Have a Clear Focus

Have you ever gotten behind the wheel of your car, driven a couple of blocks from home, and suddenly realized you don't have a clue where you're going? It's really embarrassing when you have someone with you and need to ask your passenger!

We all lead busy lives and have lots of things pressing in on us. It's so easy for our thinking to get muddled, and that's *not* a good thing for a writer or speaker. If we don't know where we're going in the message or manuscript we're preparing, how will we ever get there?

Years ago, Lee Roddy taught me the importance of a one-sentence focus statement. Because Lee knew how wordy I can be, he eliminated my commas and semi-colons. Here's just one of my "gems." Does anyone want to diagram it?

In my 2,000 word article, "How Are You Preparing Your Children to Face the Future," I deal with specific things parents can and need to be doing in order to equip their children to victoriously cope with the problems and rise to the opportunities to make a Christian witness that they may encounter in a future in which their lifestyle may be radically changed and not at all what they have become accustomed to.

Part of our problem is that we tend to want to tell or write too much on any one given topic. While I believe in the importance of providing real content, I also know that I can easily lose my reader or listener if I give too much detail.

Resist the temptation to fall in love with your words. Writers and speakers need to be ruthless, eliminating words, phrases, sentences, and entire paragraphs (sometimes even entire points in a speaking outline) that do not fall under your focus statement and do not further your purpose for the message you're seeking to present.

Create Reader/Listener Identification

It's all too easy for a reader to put down our book or a listener to tune us out. How do we create reader/listener identification to prevent that from happening? We've got to "get real." That means we need to take off our mask and be open, honest, and vulnerable.

"I don't understand myself at all," the apostle Paul admitted (Romans 7:15). "It seems to be a fact of life that when I want to do what is right, I inevitably do what is wrong" (Romans 7:21). If one of the leaders of the early church and the writer of a third of the New Testament could admit his struggles, why can't we?

"I don't mean to say I am perfect. I haven't learned all I should even yet," Paul confessed to the Christians in Philippi (Philippians 3:12).

It's so important to communicate this to our readers and listeners. If *they* think that *we* think we've "arrived" and that we're talking down to them, they're going to look for ways to trip us up and prove us wrong. But if we're willing to admit that we've made mistakes, we're likely to win a friend who will want to listen to what we have to say.

Master the Craft

A story has a beginning, a middle, and an end. Without these elements, you have an anecdote, not a story.

Your beginning needs to immediately capture your reader or listener's attention. This is best done by presenting the problem with no apparent solution. Then develop your story by showing how things went from bad to worse.

By the time you reach the crisis point, your audience should be sitting on the edge of their seats. This is the "you can hear a pin drop" or the "can't put the book down" moment. Please don't spoil it by presenting a "I came to realize" solution. Although the turning point may begin with an "ah-ha" moment, something needs to happen. And that big something is *change*.

Have you ever watched a movie only to feel cheated at the end because there really wasn't any change in the situation? Instead, you were left up in the air wondering what happened. Don't cheat your readers or listeners by not tying up the loose ends at the end of your story.

Mastering the craft includes learning how to pace your story and how to write and speak with such excellence that the readers or listeners don't have to work to follow the storyline. Instead, the master craftsman learns to so draw them into the story that they don't hear the clock ticking and don't want the story to end.

Provide a Strong Take-away

Your take-away is the answer to the "What difference does this make?" question. While stories can be told and written simply to entertain, as followers of the Lord Jesus Christ our stories need to serve the far greater purpose of introducing people to Him or encouraging them to grow in Him.

That doesn't mean our stories need to have a "now I lived happily ever after" ending. I've always resisted singing the chorus of that old hymn that proclaims, "Now I am happy all day long." It seems sing-songy and pat, and I don't think our readers and listeners will buy it.

Sometimes life is really, really hard, and bad things do happen to good people. But we can show them that God is our strength, our peace, and our joy despite what life throws at us. Sometimes the greatest miracle and our strongest testimony is of God's grace to help us hold on and work through the problem. A miraculous removal of the problem does not help us grow.

Are You Ready?

Writing and speaking from life experience—sharing your story, your testimony, of God's working your life—is certainly not the easiest form of writing or speaking. You can expect to get put to the test by the evil one. He will try and discredit your message, so be on guard. "Put on all of God's armor so that you will be able to stand safe against all strategies and tricks of Satan," the apostle Paul counsels (Ephesians 6:11).

You may face criticism and even persecution by people who don't want to hear what you have to say. Jesus did! "Since they persecuted me, naturally they will persecute you," He said (John 15:20). But He also said, "When you are reviled and persecuted and lied about because you are my followers—wonderful! Be happy about it! Be very glad! For a tremendous reward awaits you up in heaven" (Matthew 5:11-12).

And who knows? Because of the power of your story you may meet someone in heaven who is there because of your written or spoken words.

For MP3 workshop, "The Power of Story," go to:
https://writehisanswer.com/HtPEs.

2

Going & Growing Through the Hurts

And we know that in all things
God works for the good of those who love him,
who have been called according to his purpose.
ROMANS 8:28 NIV

Have you ever seen the illustration of the zebra whose stripes are unraveling? The caption says, "I think I'm having stress!"

It always gets a good laugh, although I know—from firsthand experience—that stress is anything but a laughing matter. You can't identify because you have a problem-free life? Then, as I tell the folks who attend my writing seminars, you probably haven't suffered enough to be a good writer.

Ouch! I know that's *not* what you want to hear. But Jesus never promised it would be easy to follow him. While I do not believe He sends stress into our lives, I am convinced that He allows it. Fire is the only way that our faith, which "is far more precious to God than mere gold," is refined and purified (1 Peter 1:7).

How can you go and grow through the hurts in your own life?

Here are some things God has been teaching me—again.

Don't distance yourself from the Lord.

It may sound like a cliché, but it's true. If God seems distant, He's not the one who has moved. By an act of our wills, we need to keep drawing near to the Lord during those times when we feel overwhelmed from the problems pressing in on us. (As I said earlier, problems are groupies. They never seem to come singly but rather attack us in mass.)

I remember the summer we had no choice but to put my mother in a nursing home—the one thing I told myself I would *never* do. She was only there a few weeks before I had to give the okay to put her in a mental hospital. (Mom had a dementia similar to Alzheimer's and bipolar disorder.) While we were out of town taking our daughter to college, Mom had a metabolic crisis and was moved to another hospital. Three weeks later, the Lord took her home; and just two weeks after her death, my husband lost his job.

While I knew God had not deserted us, some days He felt really distant. I had to remember that feelings are not facts and keep on reaching out to Him, even when all I could pray was simply, "Help!"

Refuse to dwell on the negatives or to live in the land of regrets and if only.

Hanging above my computer is a little wooden ornament that says, "Celebrate the Sonrise." (I need visual reminders!) Fact is, no matter how dark things may seem, we can choose to look for and celebrate the blessings we take for granted. Ears to hear, eyes to see, legs to walk, a voice to speak and sing His praises. Friends, family, church. . . . We may not have all these things, but we can choose not to take for granted what we do have and to "think about all [we] can praise God for and be glad about" (Philippians 4:8).

"Be still and know that [he is] God"
(Psalm 46:10 NIV).

Focus on Him—on His greatness, His power, His love. "His peace will keep your thoughts and your hearts quiet and at rest as you trust in Christ Jesus" (Philippians 4:7).

25

Seek prayer support and counsel of Christian friends and, if necessary, professionals.

Galatians 6:2 says, "Share each other's troubles and problems, and so obey our Lord's command." Doing so means taking off the masks we wear most of the time. Plus, we need to go a step further: "Admit your faults to one another and pray for each other so you may be healed" (James 5:16). In the process, not only will we find God's healing, but our own problems will seem less overwhelming as we reach out to others.

Search for the truth to set you free (John 8:32).

So often we listen to the wrong words. We believe the evil one's accusations and accept his condemnation despite the fact that the Bible says, "there is now no condemnation for those who are in Christ Jesus" (Romans 8:1 NIV).

A year after my mother's homegoing, the Lord clearly showed me that if I continued to beat myself up for the ways *I* felt I had failed her, it was as if I were saying His death on the cross wasn't enough. Truth is that "he is a mighty Savior. He will give you victory. He will rejoice over you in great gladness; he will love you and not accuse you" (Zephaniah 3:17-18).

Hang on to His promises.

All things *do* work together for good although we may not see how this side of eternity. We can, however, rely on the promise that "he heals the brokenhearted, binding up their wounds" (Psalm 147:3). But just as it takes time for the body to heal when it has been injured, so, too, it takes time for battered emotions to heal. Don't deny the reality of your pain. It's okay to cry. That's why God gave us tears. And remember, "Even when we are too weak to have any faith left, he remains faithful to us and will help us" (2 Timothy 2:13).

Ask, "Lord what are You trying to teach me?" and then share what you learn with others.

God does not waste pain and suffering. Instead, He uses it to mold us into the image of His Son and to teach us lessons we would probably learn no other way. He "wonderfully comforts and strengthens us in our hardships and trials. And why does he do this? So that when others are troubled, needing our sympathy and encouragement, we can pass on to them this same help and comfort God has given us" (2 Corinthians 1:3-4). That's a promise we can cling to and act on. He is a redeeming God!

Responding to God's Call to Write

Read Psalm 40; Romans 5:3-5; and James 1:2-4. What do these passages say to you about God's help to go and grow through your hurts and use them for good?

He lifted me out of the pit of despair,

out from the bog and the mire,

and set my feet on a hard, firm path,

and steadied me as I walked along.

He has given me a new song to sing,

of praises to our God.

Now many will hear of the glorious things

he did for me, and stand in awe before the Lord,

and put their trust in him.

Psalm 40:2-3

3

Dig Deeper into God's Word

1. Don't distance yourself from the Lord.
   1 Peter 5:8-9; Jeremiah 29:12-13; 1 Peter 5:7

2. Refuse to focus on the negatives and dwell in the "land of regrets" and "if only."
   Philippians 4:6-8; 2 Corinthians 4:8-9; Amos 4:13

3. Be still and know that He is God . . .
   Psalm 46:10; Romans 8:35-39; Isaiah 26:3-4

4. Seek prayer support and counsel of Christian friends and, if needed, professionals.
   Galatians 6:2; James 5:16

5. Search for the truth that will set you free.
   John 8:32; Revelation 12:11; Zephaniah 3:17

6. Hang on to His promises.
   2 Timothy 2:13; Romans 8:28; Isaiah 28:16; Psalm 147:3; Jeremiah 29:11

7. Ask, "Lord, what are You trying to teach me? How can You use me and my experiences to help others?"
   2 Corinthians 12:8-10; Psalm 40:1-3

   ✐ Write/speak what you've learned in the crucible of your life experiences.
   2 Corinthians 1:3-7; 1 Corinthians 15:58

   ✐ Be real—open, honest, vulnerable.
   Romans 7:15

   ✐ Don't write/speak too soon.
   Romans 8:1-2; Habakkuk 2:1

   ✐ Write/speak His answer—not pat answers.
   Habakkuk 2:2; Isaiah 50:4; Ezekiel 3:10-11

   ✐ Write/speak with love. 1 Corinthians 13

✐ Write/speak with sensitivity. Don't preach or lay guilt trips. Encourage; give hope.
1 Thessalonians 5:11; Isaiah 49:15

✐ Keep growing in the Lord and trusting Him.
Proverbs 3:5-6; Ephesians 3:20

✐ Commit your ministry to the Lord.
Psalm 37:5; Habakkuk 2:3

For MP3 workshop, "Go and Grow, Write & Speak through the Hurts," go to
https://writehisanswer.com/HtPEs.
\

The whole Bible was given to us

by inspiration from God

and is useful to teach us what is true

and to make us realize what is wrong in our lives;

it straightens us out

and helps us do what is right.

2 Timothy 3:16

4

Writing the Personal Experience Story

To download the MP3 of this workshop go to https://writehisanswer.com/HtPEs.

Why write from personal experience?

Tips for writing from personal experience

Keep a journal

Inventory and reflect on your life experiences

Essentials - and pitfalls - of good PE story writing

1. **Clear focus**
   Pitfall - want to tell too much

2. **Reader identification**
   Pitfall - story important to you but not relevant to
   your reader

3. **Honesty**
   Pitfall - temptation to make yourself look better than
   you really are

4. **Use 4 C's of fiction**

   a. **Characters** - contrasting & strongly motivated
      Pitfall - don't lose the reader's sympathy

   b. **Conflict** - credible problems & obstacles
      Pitfalls - can't remember all the details
      inconsequential or unbelievable events

   c. **Crisis** - black hole
      Pitfall - too emotional or not emotional enough

   d. **Change/resolution**
      Pitfall - "I came to realize" or "suddenly I realized"

5. **Structure** - effective use of scenes

Pitfall - telling instead of showing

Drawing the Story

The Hinge Story   Mountain Top Plot

   Dark Moment Plot

✐ **Flashbacks**   ✐ **Transitions**

6. **Dialogue used effectively**
   Pitfall - unnatural, stilted dialogue

7. **Strong take-away**
   Pitfall - Failure to give reader something he can apply
   to his own life

TO DO:

Use the writer's check-off list on page 37 to evaluate a personal experience story you have written. If you've not yet written a PE story, ask the Lord to show you what He wants you to write and begin working on it asap.

A Writer's Check-off List
Personal Experience Story or Testimony

	Focus
	Clear & sharp (one sentence)
	Realistic time frame
	No unnecessary characters or details
	Reader identification
	Relevant, timely, interesting theme
	Title & opening paragraph that grabs attention
	Honest, open, vulnerable writing
	Have all 4 C's of a fiction story
	Character - fully developed
	Conflict - credible problems & obstacles
	Crisis/turning point - avoid "I came to realize"
	Change/resolution - believable & not just internal
	Structure
	Show don't tell
	Effective use of scenes
	Strong opening scene - present main character & problem
	Two or more scenes - develop problem
	Crisis/turning point scene - answer from outside self
	Conclusion - don't belabor
	Used flashbacks sparingly
	Smooth transitions
	Dialogue used effectively
	Strong take away
	Answered the "So what?" question
	Avoided preaching/teaching - story must carry point
	Appropriate use of Scripture & referenced correctly
	Grammar & punctuation
	Avoided cliches, slang, qualifiers (really, very . . .)
	Replaced adverbs with strong verbs
	Removed wordiness, redundancy
	Consistent use of serial commas
	Ready to write/market it?
	Do I have needed perspective?
	Have I lived it?
	Am I prepared for testing that may come?
	Is it God's timing?
	Syntax - read manuscript aloud

For a full-size PDF go to https://writehisanswer.com/HtPEs.

What a wonderful God we have—
he is the Father of our Lord Jesus Christ,
the source of every mercy,
and the one who so wonderfully comforts
and strengthens us in our hardships and trials.
And why does he do this?
So that when others are troubled,
needing our sympathy and encouragement,
we can pass on to them this same help
and comfort God has given us.

2 Corinthians 1:3-4

5

Writing Your Testimony

To download the MP3 of this workshop go to
https://writehisanswer.com/HtPEs

Testimony

1. a solemn declaration made by a witness under oath
2. evidence based on observation or knowledge
                        (*The Merriam-Webster Dictionary*)

"We have seen it and testify to it" (NIV).
 "We guarantee that we have seen him."

                        1 John 1:2

Salvation Testimonies – Paul's example

- Begin in the beginning
  (Acts 26:9-11).

- Describe your encounter with Jesus
  (Acts 26:12-15).

- Clearly show the struggle
  (Acts 9:8-9). The Bible is silent about details,
  but we must not be.

- Turning point
  (Acts 9:17). The answer needs to come from
  outside yourself. Avoid "I came to realize."

- Show difficulties you encountered
  (2 Corinthians 4:8-9; 6:4-5).

- Avoid the "happy ever after," "I've arrived"
  ending. Be realistic about continued failures
  (Romans 7:15).

- Leave the reader with hope
  (Romans 8:2, 36-39; 2 Corinthians 6:9-10).

Do's and Don'ts for Writing Your Testimony

1. DON'T be limited to writing just your salvation testimony.

   • Inventory the rough moments of your life—the times when you were most aware of God's presence and enabling. Keep a journal.

   • Write to encourage others—to give them something to take away and apply to their own lives (2 Corinthians 1:3-7; 1 Thessalonians 5:11).

   • Avoid testimonies about things not all that significant (Wayne Caldwell, *The Wesleyan Advocate*).

   • Realize that just because you're experienced it doesn't mean it will interest others. Watch for your blind spots and be careful not to bore your readers.

2. DO make your message clear and direct, your focus sharp. You should be able to state in ONE sentence what you hope to communicate to your reader (Colossians 1:28; 1 Corinthians 1:23).

3. DO be in touch with people and their needs, not preoccupied with yourself (Philippians 2:4). Make your writing relevant and timely.

4. DO point your readers to Christ, not to yourself (1 Corinthians 2:4-5).

5. DO write with conviction and enthusiasm (Romans 1:16).

6. DO let your words be gracious as well as sensible (Colossians 4:6).

7. DO back up your experience with Scripture (or scriptural principles). DON'T prooftext (take a passage out of context), quote inaccurately, or quote excessively (2 Timothy 2:15).

8. DON'T preach! Let the Holy Spirit do the convicting (John 16:8).

9. DO write with love and with sensitivity. Avoid pat and simplistic answers, but DON'T water down the power of the Gospel. Gently lead your reader to the Answer (Ephesians 4:32).

10. DO be honest, open, vulnerable. Take off your mask. Be real. Let the reader see your struggle (Romans 7:15-21; 1 Timothy 1:15-16).

11. DON'T write it too soon. Wait for objectivity and perspective (Galatians 1:16-18). Live it first but DON'T

let the enemy silence your witness because you're not perfect (Philippians 3:12).

12. DON'T try to cover too long a time frame. Avoid unnecessary tangents or characters. Share the right amount of your life before Christ—not too much, not too little (1 Timothy 1:15-16).

13. DO be led by the Holy Spirit and trust Him to give you the right words (1 Corinthians 1:7) and to strengthen you in your weakness (2 Corinthians 12:9-10).

14. DO keep rewriting until it's your very best work (2 Timothy 2:15), and DO keep submitting it until you find a home for it (Galatians 6:9).

15. DON'T be surprised or defeated by ridicule and persecution (1 Peter 5:8-11).

16. DO, as much as possible, share your testimony in story form. Show don't tell. Use dialogue and scenes. Use the 4 C's—character, conflict, crisis, change and the Writer's Check-Off List for writing a personal experience story on page 37.

I Don't Understand

Lord, I don't understand
How Your Spirit can dwell within me.
I don't understand
How He can change and sanctify me.
But I do understand
Why I need
All You have for me.
Thank You for meeting me
At my point of weakness,
For filling me with Your power
To be all You call me to be.

6

Be Honest

I am still not all I should be.
PHILIPPIANS 3:13

"Write about what you know." We've heard it over and over, but it's true. Our strongest writing is likely to grow out of our personal experiences. That's *not* to say, however, that all writers are called to write personal experience stories or their salvation testimonies, but if you feel you are, this chapter is for you.

Reading through Acts and Paul's letters, it's obvious he felt called to write from personal experience. To do so effectively, he knew he needed to be open, honest, and vulnerable.

"I am still not all I should be," Paul admitted to the Christians in Philippi (Philippians 3:13). How important it is to confess this truth to God and ourselves. "Create in me a clean heart, O God," we need to pray (Psalm 51:10 KJV). Only then can we be cleansed vessels through which His Spirit can flow to teach others His ways (Psalm 51:13).

Recognizing how far short we fall from God's glory (Romans 3:23) reminds us to approach our readers with humility, rather than a know-it-all, I've arrived attitude. Being open and honest about our own struggles and failures creates that all-important reader identification without which people won't read beyond the first paragraph.

How open and honest do we need to be? Do we have to tell our readers everything? No! Not only would we bore them, but if we are writing our salvation testimonies, we might end up glorifying sin instead of the Savior. Wisdom says to carefully and prayerfully discern how much God wants us to share. We then need to stay within the boundaries He sets, sharing no more and no less.

According to Acts 8:3, before his conversion, "Paul was like a wild man, going everywhere to devastate the believers, even entering private homes and dragging out men and women alike and jailing them." Even though Paul knew the Lord had forgiven him, it still must have grieved him to remember the pain he inflicted on those who were now fellow believers.

For years, Paul chafed under the distrust of the church leaders. Despite the later success of his missionary tours and all the suffering he endured for the cause of Christ, he was never totally accepted by some of the Jewish believers.

It would have been natural and understandable for Paul to want to forget his past and even to try and hide it. Instead, before a mob at the temple in Jerusalem, Paul admitted he "persecuted the Christians, hounding them to death, binding and delivering both men and women to prison" (Acts 22:4). But then he went on to describe how the Lord met him on the road to Damascus and dramatically changed his life:

"Even though I was once a blasphemer and a persecutor and a violent man," Paul later wrote to Timothy, "I was shown mercy because I acted in ignorance and unbelief. . . . Christ Jesus came into the world to save sinners—of whom I am the worst. But for that very reason I was shown mercy so that in me, the worst of sinners, Christ Jesus might display his unlimited patience as an example for those who would believe on him and receive eternal life" (1 Timothy 1:13, 15-16 NIV).

We, too, have the opportunity to share our witness of the ways Christ has changed us with those who may feel there is no hope for them. By taking off our masks and being real, we can "shine out among them like beacon lights, holding out to them the Word of Life" (Philippians 2:15).

Again, we can learn from Paul's example of honesty and openness. He admitted he didn't understand himself. "I really want to do what is right," he wrote, "but I can't. I do what I don't want to—what I hate" (Romans 7:15). Yet out of his awareness of his own sinful nature, Paul was able to point others to "the power of the life-giving Spirit" (Romans 8:2). We can do the same.

But what about the evil one's accusation that we have no business writing our testimonies because we're not always living in victory? Once again, we need to look to Paul. From prison in Rome he wrote to the Philippians: "I haven't learned all I should even yet, but I keep working toward that day when I will finally be all that Christ saved me for and wants me to be" (Philippians 3:12). It is not our goodness or our obedience to God's laws that will save us or our readers; rather, it is the shed blood of Jesus Christ. We need to point our readers to the Cross, not to ourselves.

Finally, Paul realistically portrayed the difficulties involved in following Christ: "We are pressed on every side by troubles," he wrote, "but not crushed and broken. We are perplexed because we don't know why things happen as they do, but we don't give up and quit. We are hunted down, but God never abandons us. We get knocked down, but we get up again and keep going" (2 Corinthians 4:8-9).

Paul's call to spread the Good News of Jesus Christ to the Gentile world was not an easy one. He patiently endured "suffering and hardship and trouble of every kind" (2 Corinthians 6:4), but these were the very things that made his words credible. He was able to *show* from his personal experience how God would also "tenderly comfort" his readers and give them the "strength to endure" (2 Corinthians 1:6-7).

Just as Paul urged the early Christians to pattern their lives after his (Philippians 3:17), I believe he would urge those of us who are called to minister through personal experience stories and testimonies to pattern our writing after his. With God's help we can, like Paul, write openly and honestly in such a way that unbelievers will be won to Christ and believers will be encouraged and strengthened.

Responding to God's Call to Write

Inventory the rough moments of your life. When were you most aware of God's presence?

When did you grow the most? List two or three experiences below.

Bring your list to the Lord and ask Him for direction. Is He calling you to write one of these stories now or to wait? Remember, there's a big difference between writing for your readers and writing as therapy.

Study the Scriptures and do's and don'ts in "Writing Your Testimony," page 39. Write a testimony of what God has done in your life, being careful not to set yourself up as the model or norm of what others should experience.

7

Finding Our Place

*We are all parts of it [Christ's body],
and it takes every one of us to make it complete.*
ROMANS 12:5

Frequently I receive letters from writers who are questioning their call because they've fallen into the trap of comparing themselves with other writers. Convincing themselves that they don't have what it takes, they are in danger of missing the uniqueness of the gifts God has given them.

It is not the Lord's intention that we be carbon copies of one another. "Christ has given each of us special abilities—whatever he wants us to have out of his rich storehouse of gifts" (Ephesians. 4:7).

Some, but not all, have the imagination to write fiction. Some are poets. Some have the ability and enjoy doing the necessary research for well-documented magazine articles.

Others are especially gifted to write for children. And still others are evangelists, prophets, and teachers, etc.

"Why is it that he gives us these special abilities to do certain things best? It is that God's people will be equipped to do better work for him, building up the Church, the body of Christ, to a position of strength and maturity" (Ephesians. 4:12).

As always, the evil one seeks to conquer and divide. It's an old military strategy and one he often uses quite effectively in the writing community. Instead of focusing on the One we are called to serve, we can easily get caught up in the media hype and be wowed by big names and big sales. I'm not saying there's anything wrong in being a best-selling author. What is wrong is the jealousy and competitiveness that comes from coveting fame and fortune. These attitudes can also result in our compromising the message God has given us.

In *Raise Up a Standard—A Challenge to Christian Writers*, Michael Phillips asks, "Do we want to write the sensational or the significant?" He challenges Christian writers "to be on the cutting edge, not of trends, not of what's going on in publishing, in music, in video, in entertainment, in Hollywood, in Nashville, or in CBA . . . but to be on the cutting edge of what's going on in God's heart. . . . If you believe in your message, don't give up on it. Don't water it down. Don't sensationalize it just to get it published or to try to make it a best-seller. Stand firm, in integrity and truthfulness, for what God has given you to communicate" (Eureka, CA: Sunrise Books, pp. 29-31).

That admonition brings us back to where I started—finding our special place in the body of Christ and the world of Christian publishing. The apostle Paul devoted a good portion of his first letter to the Corinthians comparing Christ's body to our physical bodies. The hands, ears, and eyes are all essential. "The eye can never say to the hand, 'I don't need you.' The head can't say to the feet, 'I don't need you'" (1 Corinthians 12:21).

So, too, the effectiveness of Christian literature depends on the diverse skills of many different kinds of writers as well as the expertise of editors, artists, graphic designers, printers, distributors, bookstore managers, publicists, etc. "We each have different work to do," Paul says. "So we belong to each other, and each needs all the others" (Romans 12:5).

Although we are not all novelists, poets, or devotional writers, and few of us will ever write a best-seller, we do have the responsibility to use our own special gift to its fullest potential.

Someday we are going to meet Christ face to face, and he is going to ask us what we have done with our gift. It is my prayer that I'll be able to show Him that I have used it—that I have not allowed my tendency to compare myself with others (and find myself wanting) to limit what He wanted to do through me. I want "the words of my mouth [and my pen] and the meditation of my heart [to] be pleasing in [his] sight" (Psalm 19:14 NIV).

One of the best ways I can grow as a writer and fulfill the role God has given me in the world of Christian publishing is by developing close friendships with other Christian writers. I praise God for the writers' conference at Biola University years ago, where walking back to the dorm one afternoon, I made a forever friend. The Colorado Christian Writers' Conference that Debbie Barker directed for eight years and I now direct, is a result of that "divine encounter."

I also remember the day a young woman, new in the area, called me. Through a series of God incidents, she had found out about me and the Greater Philadelphia Christian Writers' Fellowship that I founded and direct. Again, God was at work forming another forever friendship that has changed my life. (See Sue Cameron's poem, "Words," on page 57.)

The night before Jesus went to the cross, He prayed for "future believers"—for you and for me—that we "will be of one heart and mind" (John 17:21). He expects us to love each other, "working together with one heart and mind and purpose" (Philippians 2:2). May each of us know the joy of being encouraged, affirmed, and held accountable by others who are also called to write His answer.

Responding to God's Call to Write

If you don't live in an area where there is a Christian writers' conference, consider planning your vacation around a conference that's somewhere you always wanted to visit. *The Christian Writers' Market Guide* (published every January) has a listing of national conferences and workshops, as well as groups that meet, plus some Canadian and foreign listings.

If you are not part of a small group that meets regularly for fellowship and critiquing, then find or form one. See https://writehisanswer.com/helpforcritiquegroups for Help for Forming a Group, The Critique Process, and Goals for Christian Writers' Groups.

May God bring you into rich fellowship with other Christians who are called to "write His answer."

If you are interested in a new critique group of personal experience stories that will meet monthly online using Zoom, please email me at mbagnull@aol.com**.**

Words

Is there anything more powerful?
To heal, to hurt, to destroy?
Words in my mind—accusing me,
dragging me down into guilt and helplessness.
Words from outside—attacking me,
tearing at the fragile image
of who I am and hope to be.
I struggle under their heavy weight
and fear I'll suffocate.

Not all words are true, but they feel true.
Some are lies wrought in the basement of hell,
sent to defeat those who march
in the army of God.
My Leader warned me of such warfare,
so subtle and hard to detect.
A sudden attack strips my defenses.
Wounded, bleeding, I am left to die.
Now my fate depends
on to whom I choose to listen.
To the liar, or to my Leader.

His Word consoles and strengthens me,
binding my pain and wrapping me in acceptance.
He does not condemn me in my weakness,
or require me to run on broken legs.
He asks only that I listen to Him
and believe what He says.

His truth banishes falsehoods and sets me free.
Living on the battlefield isn't kind and gentle;
it is demanding and stretching.
I must often pause and ask myself,
To whose voice do I listen?
And in whose voice do I speak?

Sue Cameron

8

Lord, I Believe, But . . .

Trust in the LORD with all thine heart;
and lean not unto thine own understanding.
In all thy ways acknowledge him,
and he shall direct thy paths.
Proverbs 3:5-6 KJV

"Do you believe God can use you?"

It's a question I also ask myself on days when doubts threaten to overwhelm me. I don't doubt Him. I *know* He is faithful. It's my self-doubts fueled by the accusations of the accuser that I struggle to overcome.

Some of you know that it took five years and rejection slips from 42 editors before the first book I wrote was accepted for publication. (See page 65.) Before that I struggled for several years to finish the manuscript. Self-doubts, and to be honest, God-doubts had me close to giving up many, many times.

The "deadly Ds"—disappointments, doubts, discouragement, even despair—were my frequent companions. What kept me keeping on?

- Promises such as Galatians 6:9: "Let us not get tired of doing what is right, for after a while we will reap a harvest of blessing if we don't get discouraged and give up."

- The very first words I ever felt the Lord speak to my heart: "Child, I never said it would be easy to follow Me, but I have promised always to be with you."

- My husband who has never told me to go get a "real" job even during times when things were really rough financially.

- My pastor who paid my way to my first writers' conference and held me accountable afterwards to use what I learned.

- Friends who year after year babysat my three children so I could go to the St. Davids Christian Writers Conference.

- The network of writing friends who encouraged me, and Gayle Roper and Anne Sirna who mentored me.

Yes, it took many long, discouraging years but that first book finally did get in print. The rest

- twelve other books including *Write His Answer – A Bible Study for Christian Writers* (see page 74) that has been in print for 28 years,

- over 1,000 sales to Christian periodicals,

- freelance editing over 30 books for others,

- publishing eleven books for others through Ampelos Press,

- thirty-six years directing the Greater Philly Christian Writers Conference that I founded,

- twenty-three years directing the Colorado Christian Writers Conference,

- serving on the faculty of seventy Christian writers' conferences, and

- teaching over fifty day-long writing seminars around the country

are the fruit of abiding in Him and trusting Him to do what I could never do in my own strength. And honestly, no one is more surprised than I am. Although I felt a call to full-time Christian service from when I was a teenager, I knew I lacked the needed credentials. I felt embarrassed by my lack of a college degree and ashamed that I was only a high school graduate.

A wise Christian recognized the load of shame I was carrying and said, "You've been homeschooled by the Father, and only special kids are homeschooled."

And then there was the day Gretchen Passantino asked me to give the closing message at the Biola Writers' Institute. "Who me?" I was definitely stretched beyond myself, but the Lord gave me the words I needed for that message and a radio interview with Rich Buhler after the conference ended.

A woman who used to travel with Yvonne Bright accompanied me to the interview and took me to lunch afterwards.

"Do you believe God is omnipotent?" she asked me.

"Yes, of course," I replied.

"Then, if God in His omnipotence chose for you not to go to college, why are you grieving for a college education?"

Immediately I burst into tears in that restaurant. I repented and was released from the bond of shame that had wrapped itself around my spirit for so many years.

~ * ~

Friends, I *know* you are not reading this book by coincidence. God has a plan for you and for your writing, and He longs to set you free from all that would hold you back.

The key is choosing to trust Him, recognizing that when you doubt, you are grieving the One who loves you so much that He hung on that cross.

I want to encourage you not to give up. If the evil one (the "defeated one" as Yolanda Powell called him in a keynote she gave some years ago) is bombarding you with the deadly Ds, trust the Lord. Realize that you are obviously a threat or the accuser would leave you alone.

Father, thank You that You know the plans You have for us and our writing – and that they are good plans. Help us to trust You when we face the deadly Ds.

Thank You for all the incredible people You have brought into my life through the Colorado and Greater Philly conferences. You know how difficult it was to postpone them to 2021 and how I grieve for those who have lost loved ones because of the pandemic.

Father, help us to write and to live Your answer in these difficult days. Use us to bring hope and healing to our divided nation.

Now glory be to God,
who by his mighty power at work within us
is able to do far more than
we would ever dare to ask or even dream of—
infinitely beyond our highest prayers,
desires, thoughts, or hopes.

Ephesians 3:20

Originally titled *How Our Family Coped with Incest* and published with a pseudonym, this is the book that was returned by 42 publishers during a five-year period. https://myfamilytoo.com

From the back cover: Childhood . . . It's supposed to be a carefree time of joyful innocence. Sadly, that is not the experience of countless children including my half-sister. Fearful she was pregnant with her father's child, Mandy came to live with us when she was not quite fourteen. *#MyFamilyToo!* is the story of God's faithfulness during the five years we sought to help Mandy overcome her father's abuse. It is also our testimony of how God helped us to Live His Answer in the midst of other challenges that could have destroyed our faith.

Please note: While I believe in the importance of being open, honest, and vulnerable, if our story involves other people, we need to obtain their permission. My stepfather was no longer living when *How Our Family Coped with Incest* was finally accepted for publication. I did get written permission from my mother and sister. I also changed their names and used a pseudonym. Since they are now home with the Lord, I am able to use my real name for *#MyFamilyToo!*

Turmoil and Change

God is our refuge and strength,
a tested help in times of trouble.
And so we need not fear even if the world blows up
and the mountains crumble into the sea.
Psalm 46:1–2

The barren trees and grey snow of February matched my spirits. *What's the matter with me?* I wondered. *I should feel thankful. Paul is a loving husband. We have two healthy children and a comfortable home.* Yet an unexplainable anxiety gripped me. I felt empty inside, and God seemed far away.

The phone rang and startled me. I didn't want to answer it, but I sensed an urgency in its insistent ringing.

"Mandy begged me to call you." I heard my mother's anxious voice over a thousand miles. "We ... we have a problem, and we don't know where to turn."

Panic filled me. My mother never called during the day when the rates were higher, and it was unlike her to come to me with any problem. Although we had once been close, more than a physical distance had grown between us in the ten years since my marriage and move to Philadelphia.

Before I could ask what was wrong, my thirteen-year-old half-sister, Mandy, burst in on their extension: "Daddy's been having sex with me! He won't leave me alone, even since Mom's found out. I'm afraid—oh, Marlene, I'm afraid I might be pregnant!"

A wave of nausea swept over me. No, it wasn't possible. It couldn't be! Those things happened only in other families—not mine. My mother and stepfather were Christians.

Numbly I listened as they began to piece together the nightmare Mandy had been living since she was about five years old. In the intervening years I had sensed something was wrong; but I never would have suspected that Harry, my stepfather, was abusing his own daughter sexually. How could he? And how could my mother not have known?

"I don't know how I could have been so blind," she said as if reading my thoughts.

"But, Mother, are you certain Mandy's telling you the truth?"

"You think I'd make up something like this?" Mandy cried.

"Shush, Mandy." Mother sighed. "I believe you. Harry's admitted it," she continued. "But he says Mandy keeps egging him on—that it's all her fault."

"But, Mom, everyone wears short skirts! Do you want me to dress like an old lady?"

"Mandy's right, Mother. Harry has no right to blame her, no matter what she may have done. He's an adult. He's the one responsible."

"I don't know," Mother said in a choked voice. "Mandy says she didn't do anything to encourage him, yet he says she's to blame. I don't know who to believe or what to do."

"You've got to do something, Mother," I insisted. "You can't let this continue. Can't you make Harry see he needs help?"

"Harry refuses to talk to anyone. He's afraid they'll put him in jail. And yet at other times, he says that's where he belongs." Her voice broke. "There, or dead and buried. I'm so frightened—for him, for all of us. I don't understand him. I've begged him to leave Mandy alone, but—"

"Marlene, please let me come and live with you," Mandy begged. "I don't want to stay here. Even when Mom is home, Daddy doesn't leave me alone. He comes in my bedroom after she's asleep. Oh, please, please let me come and live with you."

"Mandy, honey, of course you can come." I wished I could wrap my arms around her and make the pain go away. But we were one thousand miles apart, and nothing I could say or do would erase the nightmare she had been living.

"But, Mandy," Mother said, "you're my little girl. This is your home. Philadelphia is so far away."

"Please, Mom. Please let me go. I don't want to live with Daddy ... not like this."

"What am I supposed to do? I can't bear to think of losing either of you." Mother was crying. "I can't leave your daddy. He has been good to me."

"You call this being good?" Mandy spat.

"Enough, Mandy! He's still your father. He's not a bad man. He stayed with me during my nervous breakdowns. Now he's the one who's sick. He needs help."

"But, Mom, I need help, too!"

"All right. All right, Mandy," she said. "I guess you can go to your sister's, at least for a while. But oh, God ... why? Why did Harry—"

"I don't know, Mother. All I know is right now Mandy is the most important person to think about. Of course, it's hard to let go of her, but you must. The sooner you can get her on a plane, the better."

"I … I don't even know if Harry will let her come. This is all happening so fast. I need time. I can't think straight."

"You have to. Mandy needs your help. You have to think clearly and do something *now* to protect her." I shuddered. "You can't allow Harry to continue abusing her. This is so wrong—so sick."

I struggled for words to encourage my mother. "God loves you and Mandy. I know He will give you the strength you need." I hoped my words didn't sound as empty to her as they did to me. "I'll be praying for you. Please call as soon as you have her flight booked."

I fell to my knees after hanging up. "God, how could You let this happen? There's nowhere else Mandy can go. She has to come and live with us. I know Paul will agree. But why have You allowed this to happen, and what have I gotten us into?"

My thoughts raced. What kind of strain would this put on my marriage and family? How would this affect my children? Debbie was just a baby. She was too little to understand, but what about Sharon? How could we explain something like this to a nine-year-old?

I wished Paul were home. Throughout our marriage he had been the strong one. Generally, I was up or down while Paul was calm and easygoing. He took everything in stride. I needed him so much right now.

The tears I had been afraid to release finally came as I pleaded with God for answers that did not exist. Then a strange quiet came over me; a sense of peace began to enfold me.

"I will help you," God seemed to say. "Even when you don't feel Me near, I will be with you. And I promise you I will work everything for good."

What do you do when your world blows up, when everything around you crumbles? In the midst of "turmoil and change" you cannot control, how do you cope, much less manage the everyday tasks that still demand to be done?

Psalm 46:1 proclaims, "God is our refuge and strength, a tested help in times of trouble." A key word in that passage is far too often overlooked. That word is *tested*.

Problems are an unavoidable part of life. We need to equip ourselves to weather those times by building our relationship with the Lord. As we daily reach out to Him, "testing" the availability of His help with small problems, we will be better prepared to rely on Him when big problems do come.

In his second letter to Timothy, the apostle Paul affirmed his belief in the Scriptures. He said they are "God's way of making us well prepared at every point" (2 Timothy 3:17).

Truly God's Word is the lifejacket that is able to keep us afloat when we feel like we are drowning in problems. There is tremendous power available to us as we come to know the Promiser and His promises. Then we "need not fear even if the world blows up and the mountains crumble into the sea" (Psalm 46:2).

Coming Soon

in the

How to Write His Answer

Series of Books & MP3s

Articles & Devotionals

Fiction

Put Your Best Foot Forward

Going Indie

Marlene is available for

Editing & Mentoring

Workshops & Seminars

Online Critique Groups

mbagnull@aol.com

484-991-8581

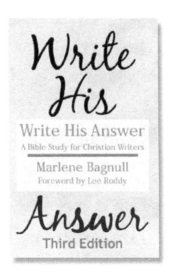

Now in print 28 years!

Practical help and encouragement
for overcoming self-doubts, writer's block, rejection,
procrastination, and more with Scriptures to study,
questions to apply the message to your life,
and space to write your response.

Check out the free excerpts
and order securely online:

https://writehisanswer.com/writehisanswerbiblestudybook
Also available as a print and eBook from amazon.com.

This has been a rich resource to encourage and challenge me
to respond and remain faithful to God's call
and use His Word as my guidance for every page.
This is a classic . . . for keeps.
Verna Bowman

https://writehisanswer.com

https://colorado.writehisanswer.com

https://philadelphia.writehisanswer.com

Summer 2021 – date not yet determined

Made in the USA
Coppell, TX
26 July 2020